FRANCISCO KRIPACZ

ARTHUR ERICKSON
FRANCISCO KRIPACZ

INTERIOR DESIGN

Figure.1
Vancouver / Berkeley

Copyright © 2015 by The Erickson Estate

15 16 17 18 19   5 4 3 2 1

All rights reserved. No part of this book may be reproduced, stored in a retrieval system or transmitted, in any form or by any means, without the prior written consent of the publisher or a licence from the Canadian Copyright Licensing Agency (Access Copyright). For a copyright licence, visit www.accesscopyright.ca or call toll free to 1-800-893-5777.

Cataloguing data available from Library and Archives Canada
ISBN 978-1-927958-50-6 (hbk.)

Editing by Geoffrey Erickson
Copy editing by Stephanie Fysh
Design by Geoffrey Erickson and Jessica Sullivan
Front jacket photograph by Ezra Stoller/Esto
Back jacket photograph by Robert Kenney
Printed and bound in China by 1010 Printing International, Ltd.
Distributed in the U.S. by Publishers Group West

We acknowledge the support of the Canada Council for the Arts, which last year invested $153 million to bring the arts to Canadians throughout the country.

Nous remercions le Conseil des arts du Canada de son soutien. L'an dernier, le Conseil a investi 153 millions de dollars pour mettre de l'art dans la vie des Canadiennes et des Canadiens de tout le pays.

Canada Council for the Arts   Conseil des arts du Canada

Figure 1 Publishing Inc.
Vancouver BC Canada
www.figure1pub.com

CONTENTS

- vi   Preface
- 1   Introduction
- 6   **Prime Minister's Offices** 1970/1980
- 10   **Eppich House 1** 1972
- 16   **Roy Thomson Hall** 1976
- 26   **Toronto House** 1977
- 30   **Fire Island House** 1977
- 38   **New York Apartment** 1978
- 44   **Bagley Wright House** 1979
- 48   **Napp Laboratories** 1979
- 56   **Eppich House 2** 1979
- 66   **Teck Mining Offices** 1980
- 76   **Arthur Erickson Architects Office, Los Angeles** 1981
- 84   **California Plaza** 1981
- 90   **Canadian Embassy** 1983
- 100   **San Diego Convention Center** 1984
- 106   **California Science Labs** 1985-87
- 112   **Khosla House** 1986
- 116   **Fresno City Hall** 1987
- 122   **Kaiser Permanente Hospital** 1988
- 128   **Balboa Beach House** 1988
- 134   **Lanyon Phillips Offices** 1998
- 142   Conclusion
- 145   Erickson Design Collection
- 180   Acknowledgements
- 182   Photo & Design Credits

PREFACE

IT WAS AN HONOUR to have the opportunity to design and edit this book on Francisco Kripacz. He had a great influence on me, as did my late uncle Arthur, who wrote the text, selected most of the photos, and created a rough layout for the book. I have had the pleasure of visiting most of the projects featured here, and they are all inspiring, unique, and a joy to experience.

From an early age I was inspired by Francisco's incredible sense of design and style. During the Expo 67 world's fair, my brother, Christopher, and I stayed in Francisco's Montreal apartment after a wonderful day at the fair with him, Arthur, and author Christopher Buckley. Francisco's apartment was high above the city in a Mies van der Rohe–designed tower, with floor-to-ceiling windows and a raised living-room floor to heighten the spectacular city views. There were elegant contemporary furnishings and art throughout, and the bathroom floors, walls, and ceiling were completely covered in white fur!

In 1981 I experienced touring New York City with Francisco while on a trip from the Nova Scotia College of Art & Design, where I was studying graphics and fabric design. He took me to see some of the most exceptional interiors in New York, such as the showroom for his friend Calvin Klein, so I could see the possibilities if I were to go into interior design. Francisco also took me to the studio of fabric designer Jack Lenor Larsen, and set up a meeting for me with the great "high-tech" interior designer Joe D'Urso. The extraordinary apartment Francisco designed in New York was in itself enough to inspire me to become an interior designer.

Francisco continued to surprise with his fresh ideas about colour, finishes, and furniture that complemented Arthur's designs. His sophistication and exceptional social skills also enhanced Arthur's career. Their homes were always designed for entertaining, and they hosted legendary parties in them.

Francisco Kripacz is a designer who will never be forgotten, and the publication of this book will help to ensure this. It was the very generous support and encouragement of Hugo Eppich that made the creation of this book possible. As well, the support of the Canada Council for the Arts, the Arthur Erickson Foundation, Phyllis Lambert, Phil Boname, and the Erickson Estate contributed significantly to the realization of this book. The photos generously donated were also a major contribution, as is the excellent design and editing by Jessica Sullivan, Lara Smith, and the Figure 1 team.

I am grateful to be able to help fulfill Arthur's wish to have this book published, and to present the fine collection of furnishings he and Francisco had hoped to launch during their lifetimes.

GEOFFREY ERICKSON

facing: Hugo Eppich with Arthur Erickson, 1982.

above: Arthur Erickson, letter to Hugo Eppich, 2005.

Transcription "Dear Hugo, I very much am grateful for your generosity in supporting the folio on Francisco's design. Your house and Thomson Hall were his proudest achievements and he was always grateful for what you encouraged him to do. I hope in some way the folio will give him the recognition he needed separate from me—but alas too late. But it gives me some satisfaction that he will be honored and remembered through this modest publication for his singular genius.

Many, many thanks to you and Brigitte for your continual support. I am forever grateful. My very best wishes, Arthur"

Francisco Kripacz in New York
Apartment, 1984

INTRODUCTION

AS ANY OF HIS FRIENDS would agree, Francisco was a startlingly charismatic individual. So many would comment, when he was no longer with us, that when he entered a room it was as if a light had been turned on. However, like Gurdjieff, his radiance unconsciously drained him and he had to conserve it where possible.

Francisco and I met at a pre-Christmas cocktail party. I asked him what he thought of Vancouver since I was curious about Vancouver friends who then lived in Caracas, his native city. "I hate it," he said. As disconcertingly impolite as it seemed, at least it was direct and honest. I was intrigued that a mere 19-year-old would have the aplomb and maturity to answer as an artist would, straight from the heart. Obviously, there was much more to him than superficial good looks.

Observing him, I was able to appreciate the naiveté and the immaculate manners of a boarding-school training, and the careful grooming and exceptional flair in clothes which suggested a European background. Little by little I pieced together his story. It seemed glamorous on the surface for one so young to have experienced so much of the world, to have learned so many languages, and to conduct himself with such confidence and noble bearing. Later I would tease him of having been a prince in a former life. But underneath he hid his need for acceptance and affection, which had been denied him due to his parents' separation.

As a feisty 17-year-old, Francisco had come to Vancouver in 1961 to visit his mother. This was an intermediate stop on his way to Switzerland from Venezuela to enter a special college course for a career in diplomacy. He already spoke five languages with fluency and without accent. He had mastered English as a very young ward of a Christian missionary family in Barbados, Italian at the Badia in Florence, German or Switzerdeutsch at the Rosario in Switzerland, and American English at the privileged Fort Lauderdale High School and a year at New York University, in addition to his native Spanish and his mother tongue, Hungarian. French he would master much later on when he would move from Vancouver to Montreal.

His father had remarried, and, under the influence of his new wife, withdrew all but minimal support for Francisco's brother, Jose, at St. George's private school. This left Francisco in a dilemma about his future. I had already noticed he had an eye for design as well as a remarkable sophistication. This, he claimed, came from his father, who was a publisher in Caracas and, in that business, a sensitive arbiter of commercial art. His mother, glamorous and impeccably turned out, relied on her son's taste in and advice on clothes, and his sartorial discrimination was already obvious in his own wardrobe. Refreshing too were his comments, freely given, on design and fashion in the decidedly unfashionable Vancouver, where, at that time, British dowdiness prevailed. In Vancouver, he couldn't have been more of a fish out of water.

With the diplomatic career seeming more and more remote, even though he would have excelled in it with his interest in world politics, I began to probe his interest in design as an alternative because of his astute observation of all aspects of design. Upon some indication of interest, I suggested he try out a design course at the Vancouver School of Art, where he enrolled for a year under Jack Shadbolt. Meanwhile, returning to Caracas for a visit to introduce me to friends and family, he found the new wife mistrustful and the family without resources. We continued on to Rio, where, fatefully, a young Brazilian designer had provided the furnishings for a new hotel on the Copacabana. The furniture was made from exceedingly rich moulded rosewood, with sumptuous suede or fine leather upholstery. We proceeded to meet the designer, avail ourselves of his extensive catalogue, and investigate the process of importation to Canada.

On our returning and speaking to friends, there were a few who showed interest and eventually purchased the furniture for interior renovations. But that would be the limit for such an exotic line in Vancouver. In the meantime, my office had become involved with buildings for Expo 67 in Montreal. We had opened an office there, and both Francisco and I felt the furniture and he himself would fare better in a Latin environment than in, at that time, a predominantly Anglo-Saxon one. Thus, in 1965, he opened a large and well-appointed showroom in Montreal for the Brazilian furniture.

With Carlos Villanueva designing the Venezuelan Pavilion at Expo 67 and a few other orders, the showroom survived. But on his own, Francisco was exploring other designers to market. He realized that Brazilian taste was too exotic for Canada at that time. He was drawn to the new Italian lines from firms that were also producing the modernist classics—Gavina, Cassina, B&B, and Flos. The premier producers he approached in Italy gave him the Canadian licences to their designs by Scarpa, Colombo, Magistretti, and Vignelli, and also the early modernist pieces by Corbusier, Mies, Breuer, Mackintosh, and Eileen Grey. He also got the licence for the well-known Aalto classics from Haimi in Finland. No one in Canada or the U.S. at that time had found this trove of treasures which would dominate furnishing design to the end of the century. He was later offered the U.S. licences, but that would have required an investment we could not have managed at the time.

By then his interest in my work had expanded and a few Montreal commissions had persuaded him that he could make a significant contribution to building design. To brush up his skills in the basics of design, he decided to take a course at the Pratt Institute in New York. He would commute, with four days there and three days in Montreal each week. He was able to study under Joe D'Urso and meet many of the top designers, like Bob Bray and Michael Schaible. He was like a sponge—longing to absorb whatever he could about design.

With the downturn of the Montreal economy after Expo, Francisco Furniture closed in 1973 after hanging on for seven years. By this time he was thoroughly vexed by the hazards of commerce with Italian companies, running and staffing

INTRODUCTION 3

facing: Erickson House, 1973. Vancouver, British Columbia, Canada.

an office, keeping accounts, and balancing the budget. So he joined my office in Toronto as principal in charge of interiors.

From then on, he realized his calling and his purpose seemed clear. The natural taste and the perfect eye had always been there, and his confidence in his own judgment grew each day. In many ways, he had been schooled well with first-hand exposure to my work. Gradually, through making suggestions to me about colour, materials, and finishes, he had become indispensable to the design team. His credo of freshness in the use of pure and ungreyed shades of colour and simplicity of form was my credo too, the Miesian dictum of "less is more."

He had in the meantime experimented on his own apartment in Montreal, where twin beds were built out of Formica-covered shells so as not to appear as separate pieces of furniture. The floor of the living room was raised so it consolidated the living-room space and provided a better view for seated guests. In the updating of my coach house in Vancouver, he used 6″ square pieces of Italian suede in a natural light camel colour on the walls to blend with the carpet and sofas as a single palette. The bathroom walls, on the contrary, were covered in glazed squares of calves' leather to blend with the teak cabinetry.

Eventually, it was through the domestic projects that my acceptance of the limitations of architectural form gave way to the extension of the architectural premise through the interiors and furnishings. That was his genius—to see how he could lift my architectural concepts far beyond what could be imagined by me. I soon learned to abdicate from the work the minute he took over. What he did was unexpected, even startling in its innovation, but a perfect conclusion to what I had started.

His vision would expand rapidly beyond just supplying the classical models of furniture for the early houses. In the large works—the convention centre, concert hall, university buildings, hospital, and pharmaceutical plant—he braved what no one else would dare. I stood behind him, though sometimes doubtful myself, knowing that in the end he would fulfill my expectations. Thus I learned to trust his judgment implicitly. In his last work, for Lanyon Phillips in Vancouver, he acted with typical panache and brought off his best work. It had been a dreary space with an

exceptional view, despite the porridge of acoustic tile on the ceiling and soupy asbestos tile on the floor. He transformed it into the most dramatic design office in the city, and sales multiplied accordingly. He used materials I would never have used, but I let him do so, with original, stunning results. I was cautious about the cheap plastic sandwich that was curved into aluminum wall frames, giving the office a winning luminescence, and about the brilliant cobalt blue vinyl floor that defied mixing with other colours, but his results were masterful. I had to command my office to speak only to him and not refer to me. They had to trust him as I did.

In the end, the success of our projects had as much to do with the clarity and strength of his interiors as it had to do with the architecture, which was often too cerebral until he took over to engage the senses. Such a talent is unique in my experience among interior designers. They invariably seem to go in another direction than what the architecture determines. When they do so, the result is not a harmony of ideas, a concordance of points of view extended to a new potential, but a diversion which often opposes or dilutes the original vision. The interiors, then, are but a dull shoring up of the architectural premise or an inconsequential excursion of their own. The rare contribution of Francisco's work to mine was a seamless harmony of thought and intention fleshing out the bones of the building into a vibrant and beautiful manifestation of original ideas, in a manner I could not have imagined. To be a part of this adventure was a joyful experience.

In this brief folio I present his major works so that those pursuing his profession can gauge the importance of understanding the motivation behind the architecture. If the final work becomes a consummate marriage of intent, both disciplines and the project itself gain immeasurably.

Parliament Buildings Office 1970
Ottawa, Ontario, Canada

PRIME MINISTER'S OFFICES

THROUGH HIS ARCHITECT BROTHER, I had met Prime Minister Pierre Trudeau and, later, Margaret, the beautiful daughter of one of his ministers, when they were married. They wanted Francisco to redo the playroom at the official residence on Sussex Drive, a room they constantly called the "special room." The rest of the house was being redone to comply with the accepted conservative eastern style. Francisco designed handsome cabinets for the music, speakers, television, books, and games for the three young boys who had arrived or were about to. The Trudeaus were pleased enough by his work, for its directness and simplicity, that Pierre asked him to redo both his official office in the Parliament Buildings and his summer office in the Langevin Block.

    This is where Francisco triumphed, for he hated the clutter of desktops, with their array of mismatched communication devices. Instead, telephones, call buttons, speakers, and video screens were set into a special wheeled pedestal beside the Prime Minister's swivelling chair—neatly off the desk but within easy reach.

    In the wood-panelled offices in the Parliament Buildings, neutral light-coloured fabric was used. The grand oak desk of Lester Pearson and elegant black lacquered

above: Parliament Buildings office, 1970.

facing: Langevin Block summer office, 1980.

pull-up chairs by Ward Bennett were combined with a set of Cassina sofas and a stone coffee table of Francisco's design.

    The summer office in the Langevin Block, across the street from Parliament Hill, was simpler because it had fewer previous intrusions. Cream walls, silver-grey carpet, and lofty proportions with tall arched windows made it a light-filled room. The desk was designed with a stone slab top and stone supports. The executive chair and Mies pull-up chairs were in cream upholstery, and the credenza was of stainless steel with a stone top. Around a D'Urso glass and stainless steel coffee table was a U-shaped seating configuration in cream upholstery—a perfect background for the scarlet and white Canadian flag in the corner. The Prime Minister loved the simplicity of his offices, especially the uncluttered airiness of the Langevin Block office.

Helmut & Hildegard Eppich House 1972
West Vancouver, British Columbia, Canada

EPPICH HOUSE 1

A FEW OF THE HOUSES I designed in the '70s were happily graced with Italian furniture by Francisco Ltd. The long, low lines, the sumptuous yet practical woven velvets for the upholstery, and the linked configurations of L's and U's for seating were well suited to my room layouts. The extensions of overlapping planes of the base, the body, and the cushions echoed the extension of building elements: the base, the planters, the rooms and terraces reaching into the natural surroundings in my domestic work. In scale and in composition, they complemented one another.

    The first Eppich house—for Helmut and Hildegard Eppich—was my first concrete house, a material that native Canadians would not have accepted but Europeans, used to sturdier structures, would. The palette was muted: concrete with wood ceilings, and velvet upholstery supported on wood trays. It was not the colour, which he would excel with much later, but the range of textures that provided the subtle richness of that house's interiors.

above: Dining room with custom planter chandelier.

facing: Living room.

above: Master bedroom with view to the garden and the Egon Eppich pond sculpture.

facing: Master bathroom.

Roy Thomson Hall 1976
Toronto, Ontario, Canada

ROY THOMSON HALL

ROY THOMSON HALL was conceived as an enormous acoustic instrument with adjustable reflective discs and absorptive banners in the form of tubes of wool, which could be lowered into or removed through the hall ceiling to tune the reverberation time of the hall to the type of music. Romantic compositions would require the most reverberation possible to fuse the sounds which the wide array of instruments demanded, while baroque works required the hall to be dry to stress the clarity of each instrumental group and therefore required all the absorptive banners.

The banner array of 2,000 items of wool tubing was initially conceived as quite brightly coloured and was left up to the artist, Mariette Rousseau-Vermette. At this point Francisco, with his keen colour sense, took on the interiors task and tackled the banners first. He worked with Mariette to propose a new palette, one which was muted and subtle, in place of the former strident palette. He picked a mixture of greys, to harmonize with the concrete walls, merging gradually with a lighter palette of creams as the arrays approached the chandelier in the centre. Interspersed amongst the greys, which reflected the calmness of the architectural volume, was

above: The oculus chandelier.

facing: The acoustic banners with occasional strands of colour.

an occasional deep wine, purple, or scarlet. These occasional strands of colour spiced the greys around them, lending luminosity to the creams surrounding the "oculus" chandelier. It was a brilliant solution, multi-layered, rich, yet calming, bridging the oval of convex concrete panels enclosing the space with a ceiling of mysterious impenetrable depth.

above, facing: Lobby with two-tone carpeting.

The second triumph of Francisco was the carpet throughout. I had originally proposed, in my naiveté, a carpet designed by one of Toronto's most interesting artists, Harold Town. This won me many points with the Board, but Francisco found it a rather homespun solution and quite freely said so. I had to go back to the Board and argue for the grey. The Board was not responsive, favouring the Town design, with the exception of one member, a patron and matriarch of the prominent McLean family. In a moment of desperation I said to her, "Look at the Board members around you—they are all wearing grey because it is the most flattering to the face," and she supported me. It was passed. Francisco, with Margaret Holland, started on the selection of two greys—one lighter, for the border, and one darker, for the ground—but both had to show off the concrete in the best light. There followed months of dye testing to find the right greys to complement the rough warmth of the concrete, making it warm in tone and texture rather than cold and earthy.

above: Custom concert hall seating.

facing: Concert view from behind the stage.

Meanwhile, Francisco was looking for a fabric for the seating. He found a handsome "cut" velour, both long-lasting and hard-wearing, from a company in New York that had plied to the carriage trades—train and auto seating. Francisco had said, "Look how well it goes with the carpets and the concrete." Of course it did, because it was grey. I had to sell it again to the Board, but this time it was easier because they realized they were doing something unique amongst concert halls—a quiet, harmonious palette to turn the attention to the music. Francisco edged the seating with chrome-plated aluminum tubing—a fine touch of restrained sophistication that freshened the endless rows of continental seating. Francisco always celebrated colour, and grey was so rarely esteemed.

Many times I would creep into the hall when a soloist was practising. As a background for music, the hall was serene, perfectly balanced without calling attention to any particular detail. The exception to this was the "oculus," the source of light

above: The organ with acoustic discs and lights hanging in the foreground.

facing: Stage view.

which supported the "bicycle wheel" structure. Tension cables, running from the perimeter of the space to the bottom of the oculus hub in the centre, paired with upper cables from the top of the oculus to support precast concrete ceiling panels. Between these petal-like slabs, the space was used alternatively for air control and for the banners of tubes, which would descend up to ten feet into the hall according to a computer program set for the tonality of the music. This ceiling—a considerable fabric artwork in itself—has since been removed in accordance with the North American lust to discard and renew.

The Roy Thomson Hall interiors are a demonstration of Francisco's brilliance. There he showed an instinctive understanding of the intention of my project, and he took this understanding to a conclusion that was well beyond my expectations. Henceforth I would trust my work to him implicitly, although I would guardedly await the unveiling of his efforts. No matter how much in doubt I was at times, I would never interfere and was always filled with wonder by the freshness and ingenuity of his design.

Toronto House 1977
Toronto, Ontario, Canada

TORONTO HOUSE

WHEN THE OFFICE MOVED to Toronto from Montreal, there were four interior design projects over a period of six years which became Francisco's responsibility: Roy Thomson Hall, Teck Mining Offices, Napp Laboratories in Cambridge, and the Washington Embassy. With the move came a concerted house-hunting effort headed by our office manager, Marlen Weiler. She miraculously found a "coach house" which had been part of the Timothy Eaton estate and which had a walled garden overlooking a ravine facing downtown Toronto in the distance. It couldn't have been better for us: two bedrooms and baths upstairs with an office between, a large living room, a powder room off the entrance downstairs, and the kitchen. Francisco's furnishing of the house was simple—the existing grey carpet would predominate with the white walls. The round powder room was an exception. It was lined with sumptuous red Thai silk and displayed Jasper Johns' "body parts" series, seven of which lined the cylinder's walls. In the living room, two paintings of Francisco's by Claude Tousignant from Montreal—round bull's-eye rings of colour—were mounted on one wall, and an 18′ by 5′ Entablature by Roy Lichtenstein hung

above: Entry and powder room with red silk walls.

facing: Living room with giant Lichtenstein painting.

on the opposite wall. A brief altercation occurred with the builder, because that wall was only 16′ long. When I told him he had to cut through the brick wall to the kitchen to add 2′ of wall, he looked at me in disbelief and countered, "Why not cut 2′ off the painting?"

The painting fit perfectly, and, together with the simple Corbusier lounge chairs and chesterfield in grey suede, from Francisco's Montreal collection, and the Corbusier table with black leather Mies chairs, it made for an elegant pad to which we could invite anyone.

The house was showcased with the opening of Roy Thomson Hall. The Premier was there, the Mayor of the city, and, from Paris, Francisco's good friend Hubert de Givenchy. From New York, the William F. Buckleys came, along with many local friends who occupied both low and high places in Toronto. It was a great success on a beautiful evening as the party spread into our walled garden and throughout our modest "coach house."

Fire Island House 1977
Fire Island, New York, USA

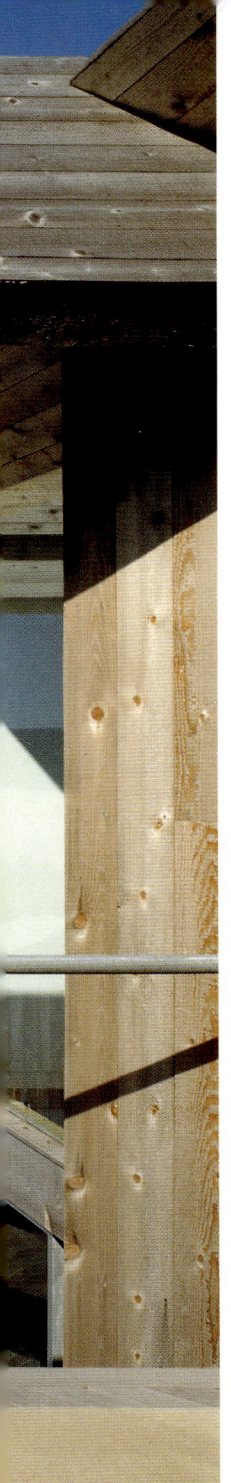

FIRE ISLAND HOUSE

SO MANY OF FRANCISCO'S friends in the design and fashion fields summered on Fire Island, and as Manhattan became more of a target for our work, it seemed logical to have a house or cabin to enjoy the summer there on the dunes and limpid sea. Francisco, who went there regularly, persuaded me to look for a house requiring a modest revision. We found one at the end of the Pines next to a Washington friend and the empty space that extended to Cherry Grove. It seemed ideal for its lack of neighbours and relative quiet. My first layout was inexpensive, practical, but not a "transformation," and Francisco said that for our own reputation, it had to be a transformation. The original shack became the chrysalis to an elaborate makeover which the locals christened the "White House." A wide, two-storied porch concealed the front façade of glass. Wide piers, angled to the east view of the beach, supported deep angled beams across the front—a somewhat inconspicuous look of weathered siding instead of limestone that earned the house its name. The grey siding concealed a pure white interior: white cotton-covered furniture, a coffee

facing: The pool and house at night.

table made of bent white slats, white Italian ceramic tile floor, white lacquered dining table, and white Bertoia chairs against the wall, on which hung the Warhol Mick Jagger series. Ellsworth Kelly and Frank Stella prints were on the bedroom wall upstairs. Francisco's bedroom had a yellow Cassina double bed; the guest room, twin black Cassinas. White, black, and spots of primary colours seemed to suit the house. But the main feature was the ceiling of the two-storey living room, which would slide open to the sky with the push of a button.

above: Living room and outdoor dining on the rear deck.

facing: Living room with roof open, and fence lowered for view.

On pleasant nights and days, you could sit in the living room and be virtually outside with the walls and the ceiling wide open. At a party, Roberta Flack sang with the living room filled with silver balloons. As she emerged amid mists of dry ice, the roof opened and the balloons floated up into the night air. There was also a notable lunch at the house to which Philip Johnson came with his partner, David Whitney, and my friend Pat Buckley.

Francisco had the property fence on hinges so it could be lowered on weekdays, when the crowds had gone, to allow for a full sea view. He was always full of ideas to which I obediently concurred. The "simple" renovation had become "the" house on the island.

facing: Dining room with Mick Jagger series by Andy Warhol.

New York Apartment 1978
New York City, New York, USA

NEW YORK APARTMENT

ALL THAT TIME WE had a number of developers making inquiries from New York. It was so close to Toronto that the habit of weekending there, and keeping up with the art scene to which Douglas Chrismas of Ace Gallery had introduced us, motivated us into looking for an apartment. The just-completed Olympic Tower appeared to be an ideal location for a New York pad, across from St. Patrick's on 54th at Fifth near MOMA. A modest price at that time got us an apartment on the 37th floor. It would later be sold for ten times the cost.

It was one bedroom, one bath and a powder room, kitchen, dining alcove, and large living room, all with 9′ ceilings. The window sills were low but not low enough to enjoy the street below. We decided to raise the living-room floor seven inches, covering the platform with grey glass without carpet. Grey slate in the

facing: Dining room stepping up to glass floor of living room.

entranceway, covered with a beautiful red kilim from Uzbekistan which we had picked up in London, contrasted with the glass. Mirrors on the farther wall and inside the deep casements of the windows would pick up the movement pattern of the traffic passing on the streets below and bring that New York rhythm right into our living room. Between the windows and the glass floor was a long, low planter of "baby's tears"—a strip of green overlooking Central Park. The cabinet for the stereo and television was of sandblasted aluminum with a black recessed strip for the controls. The same material would be used for the dining-room table, edged in a polished stainless steel round pipe frame. The Kripacz touch with the dining-room table was to crank down the end to a sidetable height next to the L-shaped grey velvet Italian sofa in the living room. He also designed a triangular coffee table out of sheets of polished stainless steel. This picked up the form of the very beautiful mauve Ellsworth Kelly featured on the end wall opposite the mirrored wall.

above: Bedroom with high cabinet and desk.

facing: Custom coffee table and sandblasted aluminum wall cabinets.

In the bedroom, the low Cassina beds were covered in blond felt and sat on a platform finished in clear lacquered parchment. The high cabinet for the television, desk, and cupboards was finished in the same parchment, all skirted by a blond carpet. It was a bedroom of supreme simplicity yet luxurious finishes. All pieces were designed, under Francisco's direction, in my office in Vancouver by Nick Milkovich, a long-time dedicated associate now heading the office there. The metal pieces were built by the Ebco company under Helmut and Hugo Eppich—loyal and helpful clients in Vancouver.

For us, it was a great ambience, inaugurated by a reception for Prime Minister Pierre Trudeau, with guests like Shirley MacLaine, Pat Buckley, Diana Vreeland, and other prominent New Yorkers, and published in the French magazine *Maison et Jardin*.

Bagley Wright House 1979
Seattle, Washington, USA

BAGLEY WRIGHT HOUSE

LOCATED ON A LARGE forested site north of Seattle, the Bagley Wright House was designed for the display of a major modern art collection and for large gatherings, including benefits for the Seattle Opera, Ballet, and Art Museum.

The major building material is a buff-coloured cast-in-place concrete. Kasota sandstone pavers bordered by concrete cover all outdoor terraces and extend into the interior, where beige carpeting is used in the main living spaces. Colours of the plastered walls and custom-designed millwork were toned from the concrete colour, giving a neutral background for the artwork.

above: Steps to entry area.

facing: Bathroom with custom vanity mirrors.

The bathroom was designed around distinctive artwork as well. A free-standing étagère displays sculptures and ceramics, and separates the bathing area from the rest of the space. It features our double-faced circular mirror design, edge-lit by a strip of theatrical lamps behind opaque glass.

NAPP LABORATORIES

THROUGH FRANCISCO'S CONNECTIONS with Renato Balestra in Rome, we met Gheri Sackler, the wife of Mortimer, of the art patronage and pharmaceutical concerns in Europe and America. They were about to build a plant in England and held a limited competition which we were lucky enough to win, to Francisco's joy. He performed perhaps his best work in the offices and reception area for Napp Laboratories. The structure was very simple—a series of concrete bents, originally of steel but changed to white concrete at the request of the client. The main reception area linked the plant to the office wing. A handsome spiral stair led up to the offices. A Greek statue of Aesculapius, the god of health, was featured in the main hall behind the double sofas fitted into low walls of the same quartzite concrete. All sat on rich plum-coloured carpets set into the marble flooring. Plum and antique ivory were the palette of the pharmaceutical plants.

It was perhaps the most glamorous project on which we were engaged. Our meetings were held in Mortimer's flat on 63rd Street, New York, designed by Francisco's friends Bray-Schaible, or at his house in London in the Nash terraces of Chester Square, or at his summer house at Cap d'Antibes, which looked over the

Napp Laboratories 1979
Cambridge, England

facing, above: Entrance bridge crossing the moat.

Bay of Cannes beyond the infinity edge of the swimming pool. A giant 10-foot sculpture of a gilded Buddha sat at the edge of the pool with a secretive inward smile defying the seriousness of anything.

The site visits with Mortimer were filled with diversions, including lunch at the head table of the Great Hall of St. John's College, a privilege I had always envied. Lunch at the college featured a private tour with the Dean to the Wren Library, raised up as a shelter to its viewing terrace, on the edge of the River Cam. Inside the library, the dark oak book stacks and carrels, named for the renowned writers, scientists, and philosophers of St. John's, lined the great reading room. There were also winter jaunts to Mortimer's house in Gstaad, where we had other friends wintering, and we would then escape the heavy social scene for the more distant and discreet glamour of the Palace at St. Moritz. The Sacklers, in the few years we worked with them on their project, introduced us to the high life of Europe—Régine's in Paris, the Grand Prix at Monte Carlo, their glorious flat, formerly Barbara Hutton's, at Place François-I, which, with its long entrance gallery and Louis XV layout and furnishings, would dazzle anyone. Francisco rose to the occasion as if this life had always been his. With his fluency in French, Spanish, Italian, and German, he was perfectly at home in the European social swirl.

The plant at Cambridge flourished in his hands, with blond lacquered desks and plush Italian seating in the limited ivory palette, which harmonized so well with

above, facing: The main reception area.

the deep plum carpets. It was good to see how such a limited palette could so richly answer the many different stations and complexities of the administrative offices. The palette was carried into the plant itself, with variations in grey carpet with plum stripes and grey lacquered furniture achieving a quiet, simple, clean atmosphere for the production at Cambridge.

The most sumptuous space was the entrance hall, which connected the plant area to the administration. The low quartzite walls containing the seating, the statue of Aesculapius against the plum carpets, the ceilings of an open lattice of polished stainless steel bands, and the walls of grey gunmetal dyed aluminum all augmented the sense of luxury.

While the administrative offices used the same cream and plum palette, the general offices off the plant maintained the palette with the substitution of a pale grey carpet with plum pinstripes and doors and furniture lacquered a light grey. The executive offices were an elegant palette of cream carpet, cream lacquered desks and cabinets, and stainless steel. The ambience of the Napp Laboratories is designed to bring a sense of glamour and elegance to the everyday experience. "Ultimate sophistication was achieved with the utmost simplicity" (*Interiors*, January 1985).

facing: Executive office.

above: Laboratories flooded with natural light.

Hugo & Brigitte Eppich House 1979
West Vancouver, British Columbia, Canada

EPPICH HOUSE 2

THE SECOND EPPICH HOUSE gave Francisco the chance to use the full application of his talents. Since the Eppichs were steel manufacturers, I had chosen steel for the structure of the Hugo & Brigitte Eppich House and other metals for the fittings of the house. Francisco came up with a chair design that reflected the quarter-circle arc of the end of the house—an ideal shape for the armchairs and sofas. He used an aluminum plate to fill in between a stainless steel tubular frame. Ingeniously, he had the polished plate ground at $3/16''$ intervals to give a vertical stripe to the steel, intentionally recalling the fabric patterns used in Edwardian furniture.

facing: Looking into the living room.

above: View from dining room into living room.

The upholstery was supposed to be caramel suede, but, because of the size of pieces required, we had to use a leather instead. The combination with the vertically striped metal was one of great elegance.

Francisco designed each item in the living room besides the chairs, including a handsome standing lamp of polished chrome and frosted glass discs to diffuse the light, side tables of polished aluminum, and a glass coffee table with a base of polished steel plate.

facing: Living room with all custom furnishings.

facing: Full dining room ensemble, table setting, and Egon Eppich artwork.

The dining-room table he designed with the top on an oval forest of stainless steel tubes with aluminum placemats and silver candlesticks, for which I was commissioned by the Italian silversmith Cleto Munari. The dining chairs were of tubular steel frames strung with fine tensioned vertical steel cables and a stainless steel compression back piece from the backrest to the floor runner. Red upholstery set off the slenderness of the chairs. The genre was used for all furniture.

above: Bathroom with custom vanity stool and mirror.

facing: Leather and steel desk in the den, with Egon Eppich artwork.

The bathroom vanity has a graceful low stool with aqua leather upholstery. The colour was repeated in the adjacent bedroom as a ribbed-leather bed cover and, at the foot of the bed, a bench, out of which the TV emerged.

In the den, the desk of purple leather was set in a wide, flat, stainless steel frame, supported by a cluster of stainless steel tubes, as with the dining table.

Francisco characteristically used a relatively neutral base colour against which he would pose clear, very pure hues and use only that hue in full intensity. The

results were always a joyous celebration of the principal hue. He seemed to find colour, throughout the spectrum, that sang with a special purity and depth without being compromised by a greying, or, as he called it, "a dirtying," to a morbid cast which has become so popular in paint and fabrics in the decorating trade today. He loved colour that was full of light but used it sparingly as if it were precious, a jewel to revitalize the blandness around it. I had thought myself fairly skilled in colour selection, but he taught me how to see colour and to rejoice with him over it.

Teck Mining Offices 1980
Toronto, Ontario, Canada

TECK MINING OFFICES

ONE OF MY TORONTO clients was Norman Keevil, for whom we had earlier done the commission of two houses in Vancouver and a summer house at Savary Island in the Gulf of Georgia—the preferred haunt of the rich and famous from across Canada. This time the head office of Teck Mining in Toronto was to be renovated. On inspection, we found that the office held the musty fragments of the different mineral deposits of his mines. It looked a little bit like the mining exhibits at the Pacific National Exhibition. I was not looking forward to anything extraordinary when I gave it to Francisco to design.

Norman had nominated his first wife, Joan, to work with Francisco. She was interested in contemporary art, as was Francisco, and the first thing I knew, he had persuaded her to go with him to Leo Castelli's gallery in New York. Francisco had an exceptional eye for art, to the extent that at gallery openings in New York it was a race between us to see who would choose the most significant work. Art became the major motivator in the Teck offices. Joan and Francisco's "finds," which amazed me, represented masterpieces in the genre, from Roy Lichtenstein to Ellsworth Kelly. The result was so distinctive that the office was renamed "Star Teck" by the Keevil associates.

right: Custom reception desk.
facing: Elevator lobby.

TECK MINING OFFICES 1980

above: Offices off reception area.

facing: Lobby colours complementing the Lichtenstein painting.

Since Teck had the whole floor, their interiors started in the elevator lobby, with slabs of grey granite leaning against the walls on either side of the stainless steel elevator doors. The entrance was like a preparation for a descent into the mineshaft itself. An arc of steel by Ellsworth Kelly hung from one wall as you entered the reception area, where the wall continued the sloping granite face from the elevator lobby. The beautiful 6′ by 8′ Lichtenstein was hung in the office of Dighem, a subsidiary, visible to anyone entering the office area.

above: Sliding boardroom doors revealing video screen.

facing: View from boardroom to lounge and Ellsworth Kelly painting.

In the lounge area, Francisco chose a fresh cream leather to upholster his Mies chairs to compliment the dark blue-purple carpet and the fresh green Ellsworth Kelly triangle he chose to hang opposite the chairs. The boardroom off the lounge area was perhaps the most dramatic space. The huge table was covered with purple leather and edged with a stainless steel tube. The Mies chairs were finished in the same colour.

A hand-held door closer opened the sliding cluster of stainless steel doors, each of which framed a narrow glass panel in a racetrack shape. The same integrity of form and colour unified the office with its distinct aesthetic—difficult to categorize except by the oneness of finishes, colour, and distinctive paintings, which complemented the choices of colour and materials.

right: View from lounge to boardroom.

Arthur Erickson Architects Office 1981
Los Angeles, California, USA

ARTHUR ERICKSON ARCHITECTS OFFICE, LOS ANGELES

IN CALIFORNIA OUR MAJOR project was California Plaza, which we won through a competition in 1981, and which resulted in our moving a branch office to L.A.

I began, at this stage, to depend more and more on Francisco for his opinion of my design. He didn't hesitate to tell me if he thought it was not good enough, and would send me back to the drawing board. More and more I relied upon him as my most useful "third eye," a discerning and sympathetic critic with the highest standards. How fertile and critical to my work were his observations at that time.

Since I was travelling between three offices and often away on lectures or a judging assignment in Asia, Francisco automatically had the role of overseeing the design in the office in Los Angeles, which was becoming the most productive of all my offices. He worked particularly well with Alberto Bertoli, a very talented architect from Buenos Aires, as well as Marcelo Igonda, also Argentinian. They stimulated each other, even goaded each other on. Francisco was not only running the office but, with his high standards and a degree of extravagance, was also making valuable suggestions—inspiring better decisions on building details that enhanced these buildings immeasurably.

above: Entrance gate to courtyard.

facing: Reception area off courtyard.

Francisco worked with me closely on the detailing of our office in Los Angeles—by far the most showy of all of our offices, yet of great simplicity. It was a former shop on Robertson Boulevard next to the Ivy, a well-known restaurant. The showroom window faced Robertson, adjoining the workshop that ran to a two-storey administration block at the back of the property, all enclosing a courtyard.

The renovations far exceeded our initial instincts and budget. We stuccoed the Robertson Boulevard façade except for a horizontal band of glass block, and faced the vertically raked stucco with panels of caste grey glass channels, which modified and brought a crisp discipline to the rough stucco. In a niche next to the adjacent building we planted a clump of bamboo, our only botanical intrusion. At the back of a wide niche at the other side was the tall iron gate to the courtyard.

The courtyard was paved with an Italian grey tile. It stepped up in wide terraces to the landing of the reception area, the second storey of which was clad in scarlet back-painted glass with a large round circle left clear for the business office and meeting room behind. Climbing ficus obliterated the ugly neighbouring wall and the wall at the end of the upstairs deck. The tiled courtyard was minimal in form and gently, rhythmically stepped up to the scarlet entrance.

Our offices, as with the whole office, were white with black or scarlet fittings. Francisco designed our two desks of lacquered "racetrack" tops on wheeled stainless steel tubing frames. On the wall hung a lacquered credenza for drawers and files, in elevation also a "racetrack" form. Francisco's office was in scarlet lacquer, mine in a "more dignified," as he said, maroon lacquer.

Our secretary was on the second level, and our offices, side by side, opened to a roof terrace over the drafting room, shaded by the overhanging branches of a large podocarpus tree from the court below. A white table and chairs allowed for work outside, or lunches brought in for friends, staff, or clients.

facing: Francisco's office with roof terrace beyond.

above: Stepped courtyard terraces.

But the showpiece was the office itself, into which one descended via a couple of steps. White walls everywhere had ledge-to-ceiling glazing facing the courtyard. The oak floor was stained black and on it black slabs of desktops were supported on racetrack tubular frames with finer horizontal tubes, all lacquered the bright scarlet. Storage cabinets underneath were black, virtually disappearing against the floor.

A signal feature, also designed by Francisco, was the indirect lighting. Red lacquered lampposts marched down the centre of the room with, at the seven-foot level, a four-part cluster of high-voltage bulbs in a black cruciform holder spreading indirect light on the ceiling. It was very smart and, as with everything he did, its strength was in its simplicity. The whole was a marvellous environment for work.

facing top: Boardroom.

facing bottom: Upper floor reception area.

above: Office with custom lampposts.

CALIFORNIA PLAZA

CALIFORNIA PLAZA WAS AN 11.5-acre, mixed-use project in the downtown Bunker Hill area of Los Angeles. We were master planners when the project was won with Cadillac Fairview as developer. Cadillac Fairview and its California partners were hard enough to deal with because John Daniels, the former head of development and a good friend, who assisted in the development of the master plan, resigned at the outset. Then Cadillac Fairview disbursed all its assets in the project because of family divisions, just after the first tower was finished. In the temporary economic slump, it sold out to Metropolitan Structures, a branch of Metropolitan Life, and we were joined by a completely new group of clients who, as developers often are, were suspicious of us in the first place. Just as we had "trained" the Cadillac Fairview team to trust us, we had to begin again with the new team from Chicago, who at first treated us as west-coast innocents, as the east often does. But in time, they developed a trust in our ideas, our details, and our dedication to good architecture. They couldn't make us veer easily from what we felt was good and sensible. The head of the team from Metropolitan became a key supporter of ours to his eastern colleagues.

above: Spiral court.
facing: Lobby entrance.

After the master plan had been revised several times and the look of the towers modified to a simpler, undifferentiated tube that the developers demanded, the only distinguishing feature that we could build on was a kind of geological approach to the stratification of the whole site. Starting from the foundation with concrete, the next strata would be of granite for all horizontal surfaces and the three-storey base of the high-rise, then a strata of stainless steel transiting to glass for the body. The glass mullions would be as invisible as possible to emphasize the glassy reflective body of the tower against the solidity of the base. The top, with its

reflective surfaces, would dissolve into the sky. All future development would comply with this common stratification.

At Francisco's suggestion, there would be on the first tower a horizontal stainless steel band at one-third of the height, but, on the second tower, a vertical strip of green glass would extend from the granite base to the top of the glass skin of the building. The granite chosen for the first tower was a rose granite, and for the second, a green-violet Brazilian granite that I had to go to Italy to select and to match with the slabs of stone. The third tower when built was to be of a beige granite.

The total of our involvement on the interiors was the main lobby and the elevators. In the second tower, Francisco was able to design the banking section of the Boston Company in the main lobby. It was, as always, handsome and simple, using the rose granite of the floor for low partitions and electrically sensitive glass for the circular boardroom. If the glass was switched on, it immediately became opaque for privacy, and, when turned off, transparent again.

facing, above: Boston Company interiors.

CANADIAN EMBASSY

THE WASHINGTON EMBASSY WAS the greatest test for all of us. It had to be open and welcoming yet fit into the classicism of Washington. We had some 20 committees to go through. Pennsylvania Avenue was a sensitive parade route to the Capitol, and our site was opposite the classical National Gallery, with its East Wing by I.M. Pei next to it. The exercise for us was to build a large enough model so we could focus on how the Chancery would fit into the fine classical surroundings without evoking a false classicism. The views to each of the monuments were carefully framed by our rotunda and colonnades.

Because we had to fill the perimeter of the site, we placed the relatively small building at the back of the site fronted with a broad entrance court. The rotunda of the Federal Trade Commission Building down the street was echoed in our "Rotunda of the Provinces." The drop-off for dignitaries was up a "stramp," our invention from the Vancouver Law Courts, which approached a "heroic" colonnade of hollow aluminum that supported only a glass vault to protect the arrivals. Beyond this, the main façade of the building was stepped back, with clipped hawthorn trees providing shade and medallion roses festooning the edges. A short columned canopy signified the actual entrance. The changing scale of each of these

Canadian Embassy 1983
Washington, D.C., USA

above: The colonnade and courtyard.

facing: Sitting room.

columnated elements served to provide an illusion of size that greatly enhanced the spaciousness of the court.

Usually the interior furnishings of the Canadian embassies are handled by Public Works in Ottawa from a vast store of period furniture. Our Ambassador, Allan Gotlieb, felt that this one should be a showplace for Canadian design and not a replica of other places and other times. But to appease Public Works he would hold a competition for the Ambassador's floor, between them and us, for a fixed amount, including our fee. The dining-room furnishings would be designed by Francisco along with the sitting room, reception area, and Ambassador's office. Francisco's scheme won—the Public Works scheme was of flocked wallpaper and antique furniture. To appease concerns of a bipartisan nature, the Ambassador's office would be in the Conservatives' blue and the dining room in the Liberals' red. Between the two, the sitting room would have neutral, creamy leather and fabric on the chairs and a champagne-coloured carpet. We would also be able to recommend the paintings from the Art Bank in Ottawa.

The dining-room table had to be sectionalized to serve groups of four, or multiples of that in larger arrangements. Francisco's table had an elegant frosted glass top edged in stainless steel, supported by a hexagonal stainless steel central column that appeared as an inlay in the centre of the tabletop. He designed his high-backed chairs in scarlet upholstery on a scarlet carpet, as a total ensemble bringing a royal presence to everything there. This was later changed for the worse by Public Works, on the demand of the Conservative Party, to a baby blue!

The sitting-room sofas and chairs followed the ribbed pattern elsewhere in the blond leather. Off the end of this room was a smaller sitting room for smaller gatherings. The Ambassador's quarters changed to a navy blue carpet with blond fabric on chairs and sofas in the Ambassador's office, and his table was made of the same Ontario stone that clads the building.

facing: Ambassador's office.
above: Dining room.

above: Waiting room.
facing: Main reception room.

Upon entering the Embassy, the waiting room features a three-quarter circle of scarlet seating which follows the circular pattern of the marble floor. An inukshuk way-finding pile of stone, by prominent Inuit sculptor David Ruben Piqtoukun, is at one side looking over the stairs that descend to the gallery and theatre below. Opposite this is the door to the main reception room, which opens through huge two-ton sliding doors, responding to fingertip pressure, to the vast outdoor courtyard and the *Spirit of Haida Gwaii* sculpture by Bill Reid. We were lucky to be able to choose or commission the artists and the work displayed in the Embassy. Peter Blake, the critic writing about the Embassy in the March 1990 issue of *Architectural Record,* said that "it could hold its own with the collection in I.M. Pei's National Gallery across the street."

The reception area itself was beautifully detailed, with inset wood floors, generous proportions, and the simple palette of blond wood and blond velvet walls inset by horizontal bars of stainless steel. Also, the coffered ceiling responded handsomely to the three separate rooms that the reception area could be converted to.

above: Lobby inukshuk sculpture.

facing: Theatre with curtain by Mariette Rousseau-Vermette.

Below the inukshuk sculpture in the entrance lobby, the theatre is a brilliant tour de force. Walls and ceiling are clad with fine stainless steel screening over silver-finished recessed wall and ceiling pockets emitting a soft, indirect light. The carpeting is dark grey, and a polished black stage the width of the theatre holds a Mariette Rousseau-Vermette curtain of polished and brushed aluminum slats, reflecting the fragmented movement of the audience in their pure scarlet seating. The cleanness of each of Francisco's spaces accomplished, as in Japan—where empty space is revered—the celebration of space. Truly, in its sumptuous simplicity it is the work of a master.

San Diego Convention Center 1984
San Diego, California, USA

SAN DIEGO CONVENTION CENTER

IN THE MID-EIGHTIES, we won the competition for the San Diego Convention Center. We tried to make this a project which would allow the community of San Diego to enjoy their own cultural events. We thought that the facility shouldn't be reserved only for outsiders coming to conventions. Always a believer in using the rooftops, I wanted to use this one for outdoor exhibits and the roof of the meeting rooms for the required tennis courts for the adjacent hotel. It was difficult to persuade the Port Authority to go for the extra expense, even though it was a minor cost for an extra exhibit space of special quality, sitting over the San Diego Bay. When they eventually agreed to it, to keep the floral diversity of San Diego we were able to plant vaulted open frames running along the edge of the roof with bougainvillea. The building terraced down to a yacht mooring on the seaside and to the historical district of San Diego on the other. The stepped form greatly softened the impact of so large a building in a key view location in San Diego, for a building type which too often by its size and heavy tourist patronage is a blight on the location where it sits.

facing: Hallway.
above: Roof supports for tent structure.

It was to be built of in situ concrete—unheard of in San Diego except for basements. It took some time and a few trials in the basement area before it was acceptable to us. But then the concrete overall was eminently successful and the few inconsistencies only added to its rugged nature. The light blond colour and the sharply sculptured supports, devised by Francisco and Alberto Bertoli for the roof and the fabric tent structure, prompted Francisco to find a very simple structured pattern for the carpets. Aside from the minimal bench seating in the lobby, the carpets would be the only furnishings in the Center. He would complement the architecture by plain fields of grey set off by panels of vivid scarlet, cobalt, or aqua. The large public assembly space at the lowest level would, in the demands for flexibility, have stacking chairs in a cobalt blue and a stage with a black lighting framework.

We had the pleasure when it opened to have Shirley MacLaine perform. Our co-architects were impressed. Shirley had been a friend since 1972.

facing top: Dynamic glass walls with brightly coloured floors.

facing bottom: Public assembly space on lowest level.

above: Tensile roof structure.

SAN DIEGO CONVENTION CENTER 1984   105

CALIFORNIA SCIENCE LABS

GILBERT HALL

Many larger buildings were subject to Francisco's input. The Gilbert Hall Biological Sciences extension at Stanford was originally planned to blend with the existing building. In a modest diversion from the original design, Francisco suggested that the horizontal windows of the laboratories should be not flat glass but rather a convex sheet tucked in top and bottom deep within the frame so the curve of the outer surface remained inside the building façade. The effect was remarkable, for the window reflections took on startling variations from the existing flat glass. Such a subtle yet effective variation!

Gilbert Hall 1985
Stanford University, Palo Alto, California, USA

MCGAUGH HALL

In the McGaugh Hall Biological Sciences extension at Irvine, we wanted to use a lot of glass to ensure the penetration of light to the labs and interiors. Francisco suggested an aqua opaque glass for the spandrels, boldly set against the golden precast concrete. But then he suggested the same colour in a vinyl coating on the floors throughout. It was a beautifully cool and refreshing touch to the otherwise monotonous lab layouts.

facing: Gilbert Hall, 1985. Stanford University, Palo Alto, California, USA.

above: McGaugh Hall, 1986. University of California, Irvine, California, USA.

CALIFORNIA SCIENCE LABS 1985–87

above, facing: Stein Clinical Research, 1987. University of California, San Diego, California, USA.

STEIN CLINICAL RESEARCH

At the Clinical Research Building of the University of California, San Diego, with its partner Gerontology, we made a feature of the entrance and the stairwell as a recognizable common hinge to both related disciplines, and thus a portal and meeting place between the two. Anticipating a master plan for expansion, this would be the first unit, rather lost in the huge field set aside for the sciences. Using entirely aluminum cladding, Francisco began to explore different textures for it. The subtle variation in depth and texture would be emphasized by the light of the region. The cylindrical hinge structure linking the two would have a pronounced pattern on the drum at the top that concealed the collection of exhaust chimneys. The spandrels were of punched aluminum sandwiched between two layers of glass. The clear glass itself had a fritted pattern to reduce heat entering the building. Floor lines were indicated by flat aluminum plates on the façade.

Khosla House 1986
Portola Valley, California, USA

KHOSLA HOUSE

IN A CHANGE OF SCALE and scene, there was a house we designed in the Portola Valley for Vinod Khosla, a senior executive of Sun Microsystems. It was a ravishing poured concrete house on top of a hill looking as far as San Francisco to the north, the mountains to the west, an oak forest to the east, and his own vineyards down the hills to the south. Moreover, there was not another house in view. The site was simply planted with California wildflowers. Movable roofs over the pool and master bedroom could close in inclement weather or expose the bedroom and pool to the stars on balmy nights. The whole house was completely computerized and governed by body temperature or voice. An elevator even responded to the bark of an older dog when it wanted to move from the basement to the third-floor bedroom.

Francisco was invaluable with his knowledge of the finest appliances, fixtures, and fittings. In the one room they let him furnish, he put only a black leather S-shaped sofa arrangement on a purple carpet. Realizing he couldn't do much about the rest of the furnishings, he concentrated on the built-ins in the kitchen, bathrooms, and dressing room.

facing: Waterfalls cascading into the lap pool below the open roof.

above: Sliding roof over master bedroom.

left: Living room.

115

Fresno City Hall 1987
Fresno, California, USA

FRESNO CITY HALL

FRESNO CITY HALL WAS to go through several transformations. It started as a memorable arch at the end of the grand concourse between the public buildings at the centre of the town. Our civic objective was to reinforce a mall between civic buildings leading to the City Hall. The new solution was a barnlike structure under a vast roof, with low eaves at each side to provide the perimeters with shade. The roof at the crest was split to allow light through skylights into the Council chamber. The split acted as a focus at the end of the promenade, much like the arch, but by the ridge of the roof. The roof was set as a traditional tile roof, only of split stainless steel piping of 1′6″ diameter acting as the channel and lapping cover. The front face of the building was concave; the rear, convex.

The sweep of the broad overhang at the front sheltered the entrance porch and balcony with two sweeping areas of stairs leading up to it. The balcony sheltered the lower entrance to the first-floor bureaucratic offices. The second floor held the lobby to the Council chamber and delegates' offices.

The City Hall sat at grade with berms scooped from the parking lots at each side reflecting the slope of the wide eaves of the roof, concealing the cars. At the rear convex glass wall, two monumental lights and exhaust vent columns acted as frames to signify the entrance to the public offices at the north face of the building.

Francisco and Alberto worked on the refinement of the roof form and the interiors while I left for the other offices, and returned to critique and approve their work. The stainless steel was carried into the walls of the lobby with polished grey and white terrazzo and blond carpeting.

far left: Monumental entry lights in exhaust vent columns.

facing: Light-filled lobby.

above: Stairs to Council chamber lobby.

above, facing: Council chamber.

The Council chamber itself, with its high skylight, lacquered blond furniture, and clear cerulean carpet and upholstery, responded to Francisco's freshness of colour. He had always eschewed paint, as did I, as a material, unless it was enamel or lacquer.

Kaiser Permanente Hospital 1988
Baldwin Park, California, USA

KAISER PERMANENTE HOSPITAL

FRANCISCO'S MOST DIFFICULT assignment was the Baldwin Park Hospital for Kaiser Permanente. It was on the route to Las Vegas outside of Pasadena. We designed an extensive parking facility as a four-storied wall around the perimeter of the site to shield it from traffic noise. Inside would be a garden and a lake, out of which the main bed facility would rise in a sloping, curved mass. This would give the patients a quiet, sheltered, recreational garden.

Francisco and Alberto worked on the exterior colours of the series of buildings, with a sunny yellow for the main entrance. Blond finishes and polished steel dominated the interior palette. The carpets throughout were a soft light grey with nodes of violet and blue or other strong colours in specific locations to designate the different departments of the building.

As with the Convention Center in San Diego, Francisco and Alberto, Venezuelan and Argentinian, worked well together, challenging each other through colour and form until the whole complex of buildings worked together as a harmonious family of buildings. It had none of the institutional look of most hospitals.

right: Lobby.

facing: The curvilinear façade with lake and garden.

124 KAISER PERMANENTE HOSPITAL 1988

above: The carpeting coloured to designate departments.

right: Cafeteria.

facing: Colourful entrance canopy.

They had made it more playful, inviting, and recreational—a definite contribution to the rethinking of hospitals as a place where the patient's health is helped by the harmonious relationship of building, interior design, and landscape. Each department of the hospital—clinic, dormitories, research, operating room, etc.—had its own distinct palette simply introduced, offsetting the usual blandness of self-conscious coloration in health facilities.

When, unannounced, we visited the hospital, our reception was warm indeed. The clerk said, "This must be the only hospital in America where we can ask our patients, 'Which type of room would they prefer—the garden-view or the mountain-view!'"

Balboa Beach House 1988
Newport Beach, California, USA

BALBOA BEACH HOUSE

FOR THE KARATZ HOUSE on Balboa Beach, Barbara Barry was brought in to select the furniture and fabrics, but Francisco still had the say in the kitchen and all the bathrooms. With glass and glass block for all the walls and the floor and ceiling over the courtyard, the house radiated light. Where walls were solid, like the fireplace wall in the living room, they were of a French limestone, as were the floors and the outside walls enclosing the courtyard. The entrance gate was finished with stainless steel doors and fittings with a simple pattern of convex circles. A reflecting pool extended the living-room floor at knee level and cooled breezes entering off the hot sands.

facing: Patio with doors onto beach.

left: Outdoor dining table connected to water feature.

above: Patterned steel entrance door.

BALBOA BEACH HOUSE 1988

above: Glass block wall in custom stainless steel kitchen.

facing: Custom steel vanity, illuminated mirror, and shower.

The kitchen was to carry out the theme of a glass house, from the Maison de Verre in Paris, with frosted glass for cupboard doors and drawer faces, and granite for countertops. The owners were nervous about glass, so it was finished in stainless steel instead. At least the bathrooms could be stainless steel and glass as Francisco had wanted, and the children's bathrooms lined with frosted glass and free glass basins on glass counters—the result was a very soft aqua colour to the glass.

Lanyon Phillips Offices 1998
Vancouver, British Columbia, Canada

LANYON PHILLIPS OFFICES

FRANCISCO'S LAST WORK—one that was the most difficult and challenging but produced a solution that was exceptionally imaginative—was the offices of Lanyon Phillips, an important advertising firm in Vancouver. Our first view of the office space was depressing: cheap acoustic tile ceiling, linoleum flooring, overbuilt wood framing, dark offices with a magnificent view of the sea and mountains beyond. The deep offices needed the penetration of light to the work areas in the rear. This included the workstations for senior personnel along the window; presentation rooms for clients and for designers' conferencing, next; and, finally, the workstations for technical staff and accounting staff in the back area close to general filing.

Francisco found a brilliant blue vinyl tile, which I cautioned would be too bright to be matched by any other colour. Then he found a ribbed plastic sandwich panel, a poly-gel polycarbonate panel that I had rejected. He liked it because of the way it picked up the light and wanted to use it. By using it horizontally on T-shaped curved aluminum mullions, he not only added to its strength but also brought light, refracted into many strips of colour, into the interior meeting rooms. That determined the rest of the palette. The acoustic tile on the ceiling was replaced with

hung panels of stainless steel screening. The modular 4-desks, files, and low walls radiated off central columns, which acted as lighting standards to the clusters of workstations. The workstations along the perimeter windows were finished in a Japanese silver vinyl, the privacy screens in the ribbed translucent plastic. The partners' offices were in the same finishes but with freestanding desks and credenzas in the silver vinyl. Therefore, silver in dark and light tones became the foil for the brilliant cobalt of the floor. The other foil was a silvery lettuce green for the seating arrangement in the staff cafeteria.

Every shiny surface reflected its light on the floor, making it seem like a blue sea. At the entrance, a reception desk of stainless steel mesh, designed by Francisco with stainless steel edging, stood in front of the logo of the company projected onto frosted glass. Opposite the desk were two triangular benches of polished stainless steel supporting air cushions of backlit translucent vinyl sheets over transparent bubble wrap. Such was the ingenuity of his thinking—using banal materials to achieve a lustre beyond its evident potential.

facing: Reception with custom desk and illuminated translucent seating.

above: Cafeteria with custom dining table.

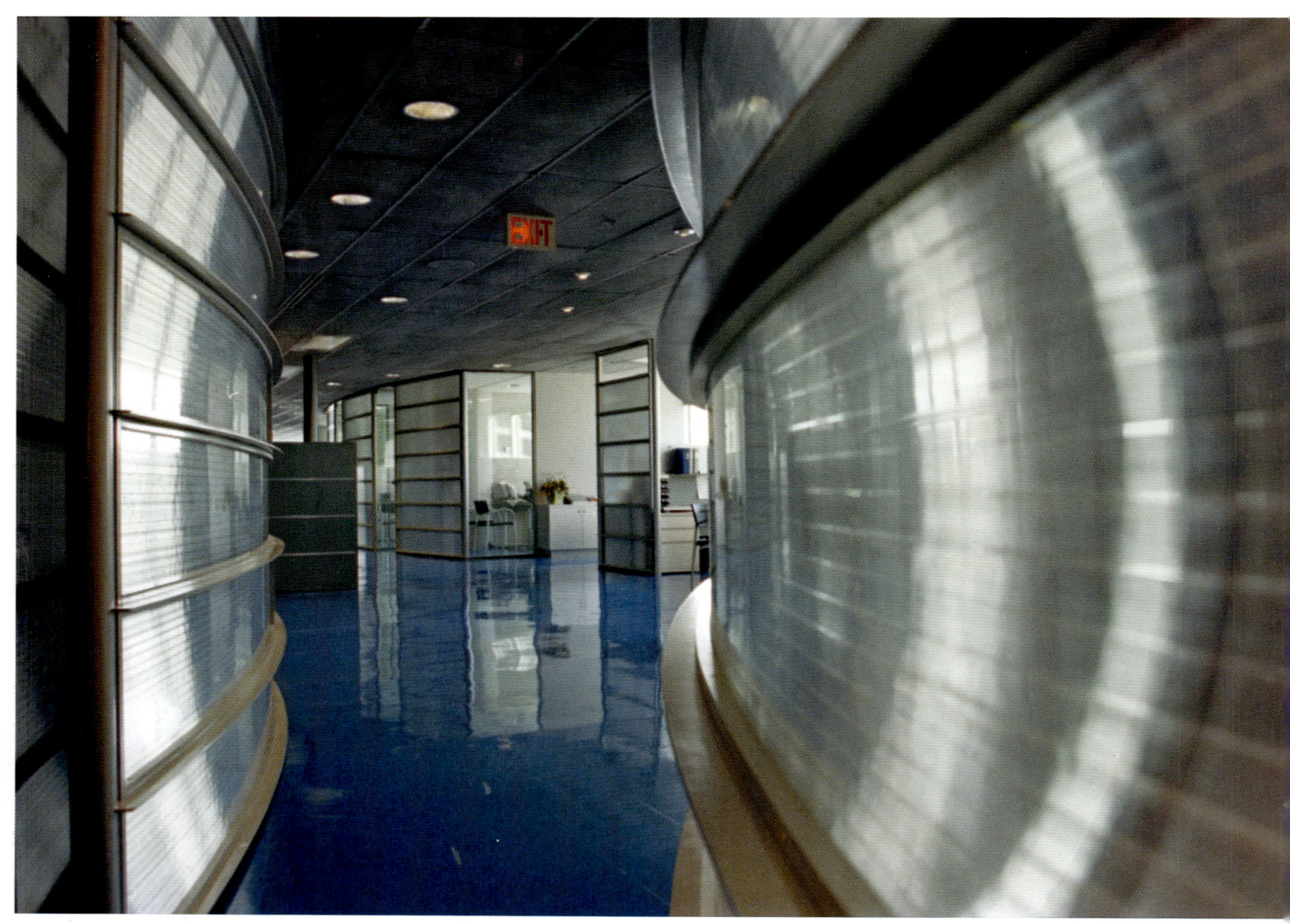

above: Light reflecting on privacy screens.

facing: Conference room.

CONCLUSION

AT A YOUNG 58 YEARS of age, Francisco sadly passed away on March 3, 2000. It was a shock and great loss to all who knew him, worked with him, and loved him. I was always aware of his low self-esteem and delicate health and felt he only needed work that would lift his self-esteem, and recognition for it. But I was using my experience to interpret his, which one can never do—his need for recognition was far more profound than mine, and his self-esteem almost nonexistent. Physically, he could dazzle anyone with that brilliant smile that could captivate instantly, but, unknown to his admirers, it betrayed a feeling of failure, of accomplishing nothing. This, to me, was inconceivable because the contrary evidence was so great.

My greatest surprise and delight was when he was publicly recognized and feted as the "Designer of the Year" by *Interiors* magazine in January 1985. I was so delighted for him and felt that this was, at last, the affirmation he needed to boost his confidence. But nothing, I guess, could pull him out of the pit of despair instilled by his early youth buffeted from school to school, country to country, when he needed the stability, reassurance, and love of his family.

I was moved to honour him with this modest publication because his contribution was not fully appreciated. Because I overshadowed him in my employees' minds, he was often ignored by the office. Even though I refused to comment on his decisions when he took on a project, I would still be asked, by my staff, to make a decision, and would have to insist that they refer to him.

He never felt completely accepted by his peers, although the standards he set himself—whether in design, in hiring personnel, or in critical assessment of art, music, conversation, public affairs—were unusually high. Of course, in the culinary and hospitality field he was full of knowledge because he knew every good restaurant or hotel and had friends everywhere. Being with him, exploring the remote locations of the world, was a joy. He knew how to have fun, how to be serious, when to make an impeccable judgment or to keep silent. He inspired me to treat life as a glorious adventure to be savoured lustily. To be part of that was to be a privileged epicurean of worldly pleasure. But he was also deeply spiritual. That streak of Hungarian in his birthright gave him confidence in his intuition that ruled events, places, and people. He had an unswerving loyalty to friends but could be unforgiving if betrayed. Joy and despair vacillated in his outlook, and, towards the end, the latter, for no apparent reason, took over. As many were to remark at the services for him, when he entered a room it was as if a light were turned on—so radiant was he—and, just as suddenly, that light was taken from us.

ERICKSON DESIGN COLLECTION©

INTEGRAL TO THE SUCCESS of the interiors Arthur Erickson designed with Francisco Kripacz were the unique furnishings they designed for these spaces. So here we present a select gallery of their elegant and timeless designs, most of which are being made available and presented as a collection for the first time.

EMBASSY COLLECTION

DESIGNS FROM
THE CANADIAN EMBASSY,
WASHINGTON, D.C.

Embassy Sofa 1986
Manufactured by Nienkamper.
Made in sections of ribbed leather or quilted fabric upholstery.

Embassy Lounge Chair 1986
Manufactured by Nienkamper.
Made of ribbed leather or quilted fabric upholstery.

151

facing
Embassy Dining Chair 1986
Manufactured by Nienkamper.
Mirror-polished chrome frame, with ribbed leather or fabric upholstery.

above
Embassy Dining Table 1986
Manufactured by Nienkamper.
Made with a frosted glass top edged in stainless steel, and supported by a hexagonal base which appears as an inlay in the table top. It can be combined with other sections to make long tables.

ERICKSON DESIGN COLLECTION

facing top
Embassy Side Table 1986
Manufactured by Nienkamper.
A hexagonal design made in stainless steel or marble.

facing bottom, above
Embassy Armchair 1986
Manufactured by Nienkamper.
Made of ribbed leather or fabric upholstery.

EPPICH 2 COLLECTION

DESIGNS FROM
THE HUGO & BRIGITTE
EPPICH HOUSE

Eppich 2 Armchair & Sofa 1989
Manufactured by Ebco Group of Companies.
Striped aluminum plate between stainless steel
tubular frames, and leather upholstery.

Eppich 2 Glass Coffee Table 1989
Manufactured by Ebco Group of Companies.
Chrome-plated steel tubes sit on a base of
polished steel, with a glass top.

Eppich 2 Dining Chair 1989
Manufactured by Ebco Group of Companies.
Tubular steel frames strung with fine tensioned
vertical steel rods secured with gold-plated screws,
and a stainless steel compression back piece.

Eppich 2 Oval Dining Table 1989
Manufactured by Ebco Group of Companies.
Chrome-plated steel tubes sit on an oval base
of polished steel, with a granite top.

Eppich 2 Placemat 1989
Manufactured by Ebco Group of Companies.
Polished and satin-finished aluminum.

above
Eppich 2 Pedestal Table 1989
Manufactured by Ebco Group of Companies.
Chrome-plated steel tubes sit on a base of steel,
with a polished and satin-finished aluminum top.

facing
Eppich 2 Round Dining Table 1989
Manufactured by Ebco Group of Companies.
Polished steel with ovals cut out of the column base, and a glass top.

Eppich 2 Side Table 1989
Manufactured by Ebco Group of Companies.
Chrome-plated steel tubes sit on a base of steel,
with a polished and satin-finished aluminum top.

Eppich 2 Steel Coffee Table 1989
Manufactured by Ebco Group of Companies.
Chrome-plated steel tubes sit on a base of steel,
with a polished and satin-finished aluminum top.

Eppich 2 Stool 1989
Manufactured by Ebco Group of Companies.
Chrome-plated steel tubes sit on a base of
polished steel, with leather upholstery.

Eppich 2 Desk 1989
Manufactured by Ebco Group of Companies.
Leather top set in a wide, flat, stainless steel frame, supported by a cluster of chrome-plated steel tubes on a base of polished steel.

above
Eppich 2 Chandelier 1989
Manufactured by Ebco Group of Companies.
Glass and chrome-plated steel.

facing
Eppich 2 Lamp 1989
Manufactured by Ebco Group of Companies.
Polished chrome and frosted glass discs.

ERICKSON CLASSICS

SELECT FURNISHINGS
FROM THE COLLECTION

facing
Erickson Tables 1986–98
Erickson-Kripacz version with steel legs, clear and frosted glass tops and shelves. Also available in round or oval, as well as in coffee-table height.

above
Original prototype table by Christopher and Geoffrey Erickson, 1986.

above
Erickson Mirrors 1979
Circular or racetrack oval designs, wall-mounted or free-standing, with double-faced mirrors edge-lit by a strip of theatrical lamps. An opaque glass collar encases the lights for diffused illumination.

facing
Erickson Candlesticks 1982
Manufactured by Cleto Munari.
Sterling silver.

ACKNOWLEDGEMENTS

I wish to gratefully acknowledge the support of the following:
Hugo & Brigitte Eppich
The Arthur Erickson Foundation
Phyllis Lambert
Phil Boname
The Erickson Estate
Brigitte Desrochers
Canada Council for the Arts

Special thanks to the following contributors:
Alan Bell
Christopher Erickson
Jeff Kew
Keith Loffler
Emily Erickson McCullum
Nick Milkovich
Richard Nadeau
Klaus & Ottilie Nienkamper
Simon Scott
Emmanuel St. Juste
Ann Videriksen

Thank you to the following donors for their generous contributions:
Diego Arria
Mrs. John Daniels
Carolyn Druion
Robert Eichler
Hugo Eppich
Shirlee Fonda
Jasmine Forman
John & Joan Hotchkis
Lynda Palevsky
Nick & Patty Skouras
Felisa Vanoff
Tim Vreeland

Francisco Kripacz (left) with furniture manufacturer Klaus Nienkamper, 1985.

Many photos were generously donated by:
Roger Brooks
Dick Busher
Geoffrey Erickson
Timothy Hursley
Marcelo Igonda
Yousuf Karsh Foundation
Jane Lidz
Norman McGrath
Klaus Nienkamper
Ray Paulsen
Simon Scott
Dave Smith
Fiona Spalding-Smith

Custom Design Manufacturers:
Embassy Series–Nienkamper
Eppich 2 Series & other furniture–Ebco Group of Companies
Erickson Candlesticks–Cleto Munari

Available exclusively to designers + collectors.
For more information about the collection, please visit:
arthurerickson.com/erickson-design-collection

For more information about the Arthur Erickson Foundation, please visit: aefoundation.ca

PHOTO & DESIGN CREDITS

Interior design by Francisco Kripacz and Arthur Erickson with additional design credits listed below. Dates shown are design dates only. Numbers listed with photo credits refer to page numbers.

Prime Minister's Offices
Parliament Buildings, 1970
Design: Nick Milkovich
Photos: Fiona Spalding-Smith (6, 8)

Prime Minister's Offices
Langevin Block, 1980
Design: Keith Loffler, Fred Allin
Photos: Fiona Spalding-Smith (9)

Eppich House 1, 1972
Design: Nick Milkovich
Photos: Dick Busher © 1979 (10), Simon Scott (12–15)

Roy Thomson Hall, 1976
Design: Keith Loffler, Margaret Holland, Anne Vezina
Photos: Fiona Spalding-Smith (18–22, 24–25), Tim Hursley (16, 23)

Toronto House, 1977
Photos: Norman McGrath (26–29)

Fire Island House, 1977
Design: Nick Milkovich, George Hunter
Photos: Ezra Stoller/Esto (30–37)

New York Apartment, 1978
Design: Keith Loffler, Fred Allin, Nick Milkovich
Photos: Norman McGrath (38–43)

Bagley Wright House, 1979
Design: Nick Milkovich, Inara Kundzins, Allan Cheng, Bob Hoshide, Sandra Fraser
Photos: Roger Brooks (46), Tim Hursley (44, 47)

Napp Laboratories, 1979
Design: Alberto Zennaro, Fred Allin, Pui-To Chau, Peter Clewes, Richard Coombs, Rudy Wallman
Photos: Tim Hursley (48, 50–55)

Eppich House 2, 1979
Design: Nick Milkovich, Inara Kundzins
Photos: Roger Brooks (59), Geoffrey Erickson (56-58, 60, 64-65), Robert Pisano (63)

Teck Mining Offices, 1980
Design: Ralph Bergman, Anne Vezina
Photos: Norman McGrath (66-75)

Arthur Erickson Architects Office, Los Angeles, 1981
Design: Randolph Jefferson, Marcelo Igonda
Photos: Marvin Rand (76-80, 82-83), Marcelo Igonda (81)

California Plaza, 1981
Design: Randolph Jefferson, Yasuo Muramatsu, Marcelo Igonda, Howard Kurushima, Joseph Collins
Photos: © Richard J.W. Wright (84), Marcelo Igonda (86-87), Alex Vertikoff (88-89)

Canadian Embassy, 1983
Design: Keith Loffler, Barbara Vogel, Fred Allin, Anne Vezina
Photos: Paul Warchol (90, 93-95, 97, 99), Ricardo Castro (92), Erickson Estate Collection (96), Richard Bryant (98)

San Diego Convention Center, 1984
Design: Alberto Bertoli, Yasuo Muramatsu, Richard Stevens, Michael Kan, Daynard Tullis
Photos: Peter Aaron (100, 102, 104-105), Erickson Estate Collection (103)

California Science Labs
Gilbert Hall, 1985
Design: Joseph Collins, Alberto Bertoli, Elizabeth Widerhorn
Photos: Geoffrey Erickson (106, 108)

California Science Labs
McGaugh Hall, 1986
Design: Joseph Collins, James Matson, Timothy Lambert
Photos: Dave Smith (109)

California Science Labs
Stein Clinical Research, 1987
Design: Joseph Collins, James Matson, Jay Hughey
Photos: Erickson Estate Collection (110), Geoffrey Erickson (111)

Khosla House, 1986
Design: Marcelo Igonda, Daynard Tullis, Paul Murdoch
Photos: Russell Abraham (112, 115 top), Roger Brooks (114, 115 bottom)

Fresno City Hall, 1987
Design: Alberto Bertoli, Susan Hubbard Oakley
Photos: Jane Lidz (116, 119, 121), Roger Brooks (118 right), Mark Darley/Esto (118 left), Erickson Estate Collection (120)

Kaiser Permanente Hospital, 1988
Design: Alberto Bertoli, Daynard Tullis
Photos: Warren Air Video & Photography (122), Erickson Estate Collection (124, 125 bottom, 126), © Richard J.W. Wright (125 top), Wayne Thom (127)

Balboa Beach House, 1988
Design: Paul Murdoch, Daynard Tullis, Marcelo Igonda
Photos: Tim Street-Porter (128, 130, 131 left, 132), Erickson Estate Collection (131 right, 133)

Lanyon Phillips Offices, 1998
Design: Nick Milkovich, Inara Kundzins
Photos: Roger Brooks (134-37, 139-41), Erickson Estate Collection (138)

Erickson Design Collection
Photos: Ray Paulsen (144), Geoffrey Erickson (146, 156, 161-62, 165-69, 171-73, 176, 178), Erickson Estate Collection (148), Thomas Lamb (149, 151, 152 top, 153, 154 top, 155), Paul Warchol (150, 152 bottom, 154 bottom), Robert Pisano (158, 163-64, 170, 179), Robert Kenney (159), Roger Brooks (160, 177), Tim Hursley (174)

Photo: Hugo Eppich (vi)
Photo: Yousuf Karsh (viii)
Photo: Simon Scott (5)
Photo: Ray Paulsen (181)

All care has been given to ensure the accuracy of image credits.